FIRST LEARNING LIBRARY

SMALL ANIMALS

Written by Andrew Branson

Illustrated by Stephen Holmes

KIBWORTH
—BOOKS—

Shrew

Shrews are busy little animals which live among fallen leaves and long grass.

The pygmy shrew is no longer than your finger.

Common shrew

Pygmy shrew

Shrews have tiny ears

Shrews have long pointed noses

Their whiskers help them to feel for food

When two shrews
meet, they may fight
fiercely over territory!

A shrew eats more
than its own weight
in food every day.

A shrew has up to
ten babies at once.

When baby
shrews follow their
mother, they hold on
to each other so they
do not get lost.

Hummingbird

Giant hummingbird

Hummingbirds are tiny and brightly coloured. They live in the tropical forests of the Americas.

Marvellous spatuletail

They can hover in the air and even fly backwards.

Long bill for reaching into flower

Drinks nectar

Most kinds of hummingbirds drink nectar from flowers, but some eat insects.

Eats insects

Bee hummingbird

Their wings beat so fast that they make a humming noise

The bee hummingbird is the smallest bird in the world. Its nest is as small as a thimble!

Snail

Shell

Snails are small animals with
hard shells. They curl inside
their shells for safety.

**Snails have
one foot**

**Snails have tiny
teeth so they can
chew their food**

They feed
on leaves and
rotting plants.

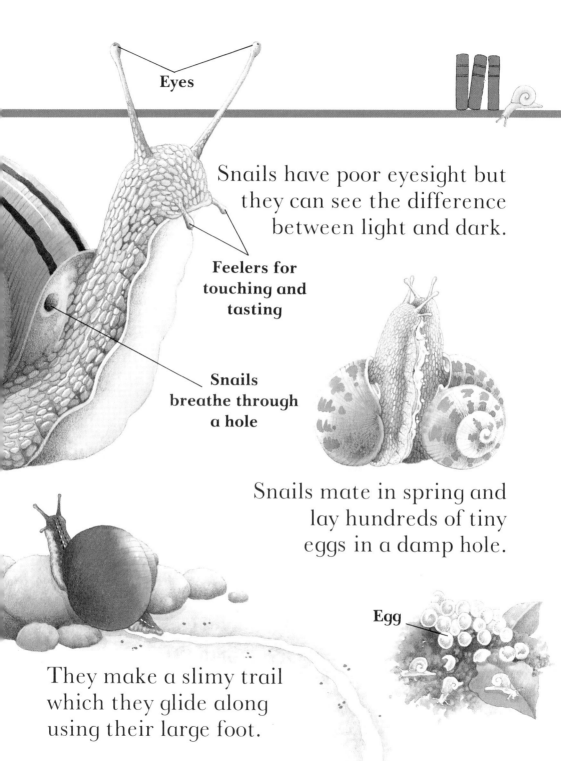

Eyes

Snails have poor eyesight but they can see the difference between light and dark.

Feelers for touching and tasting

Snails breathe through a hole

Snails mate in spring and lay hundreds of tiny eggs in a damp hole.

Egg

They make a slimy trail which they glide along using their large foot.

Butterfly

Butterflies are insects with large, beautifully marked wings.

There are many different kinds of butterflies.

Wing

Feelers

They use their long tongues to drink nectar from flowers.

A butterfly's tongue is like a straw

Egg

Butterflies lay eggs on leaves.

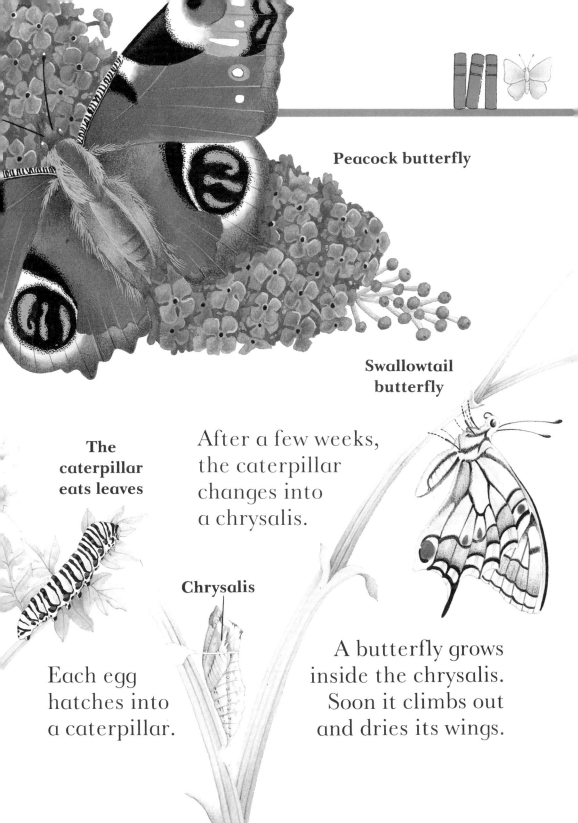

Peacock butterfly

Swallowtail butterfly

The caterpillar eats leaves

After a few weeks, the caterpillar changes into a chrysalis.

Chrysalis

Each egg hatches into a caterpillar.

A butterfly grows inside the chrysalis. Soon it climbs out and dries its wings.

Harvest mouse

Harvest mice are very small.
You can tell them from
other mice because
they have rounded
faces, small ears
and orange and
white fur.

**Tail loops
round
stalks**

**Their feet
help them to
grip the
stalk**

Harvest mice
climb around
on tall grasses.

**Long front teeth
for gnawing
food**

Harvest mice like
to eat seeds, grain,
grass, blackberries
and even small eggs.

Blades of grass are woven around stalks

Barn owl

Harvest mice are very good at building nests.

Mothers can have five babies at once. The baby mice have darker fur than the adults.

Baby mouse

Harvest mice hide in the grass from hungry owls!

Frog

Frogs can live in water and on land.

Smooth skin

Long sticky tongue to catch insects

Frogs can jump a long way. They use their back legs to push themselves high into the air.

Some male frogs puff out their chins and sing to attract a female!

Webbed feet for swimming

There are many kinds of frogs. Not all of them live by water.

Tree frog

Suckers for clinging to stems

Poison arrow frog

Desert frog

Most female frogs lay their eggs in water. The eggs hatch into tadpoles.

Young frogs

Eggs, called frogspawn

Tadpoles

Legs start to grow

Ant

Ants are tiny insects. They build amazing underground nests with many different tunnels and rooms.

Queen ant

One ant is bigger than the others. She is called the queen and lays all the eggs.

Worker ant brings food

Worker ant

Larvae

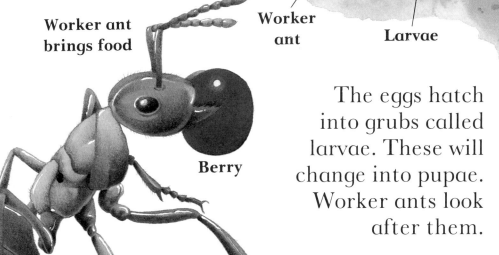

Berry

The eggs hatch into grubs called larvae. These will change into pupae. Worker ants look after them.

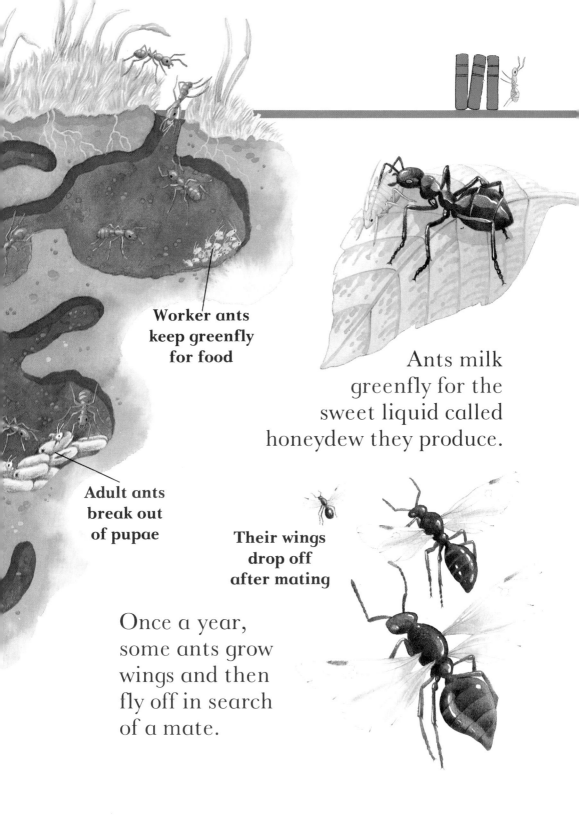

Worker ants keep greenfly for food

Adult ants break out of pupae

Ants milk greenfly for the sweet liquid called honeydew they produce.

Their wings drop off after mating

Once a year, some ants grow wings and then fly off in search of a mate.

Stickleback

Ten-spined stickleback

Sticklebacks are tiny fish not much longer than your finger. They live in ponds and streams and even in the sea.

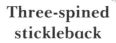

Three-spined stickleback

They feed on insects and small grubs.

Spine

In spring, the chin and belly of the three-spined male turn red

The male builds a nest from weeds.
Sticky threads from his body
glue the weeds together.

**The male makes
a tunnel through
the nest**

Egg

He leads the female
into the nest where
she lays her eggs.

**The eggs hatch
into fish**

The male protects the eggs
and young, even from fish
much bigger than himself.

**His spines
stand on end to
look frightening**

Ladybird

Ladybirds are brightly coloured insects. They keep their wings tucked inside wing cases.

Wing cases

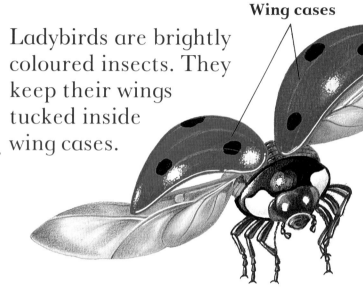

The bright colours warn animals that ladybirds are poisonous

When a ladybird flies, it opens its wing cases and holds them above its body.

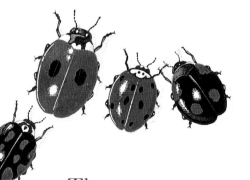

An angry ladybird squirts nasty-tasting liquid from its joints

There are more than 3,000 types of ladybird.

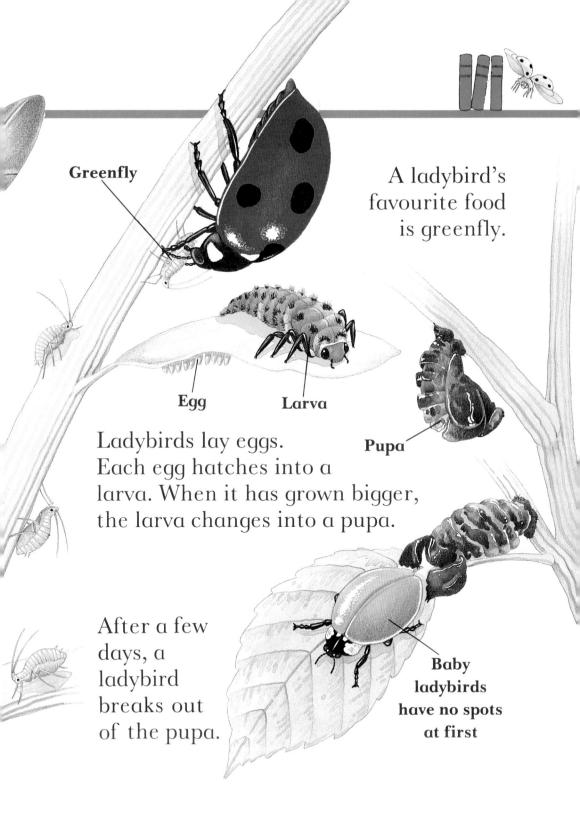

Greenfly

A ladybird's favourite food is greenfly.

Egg

Larva

Pupa

Ladybirds lay eggs.
Each egg hatches into a
larva. When it has grown bigger,
the larva changes into a pupa.

After a few
days, a
ladybird
breaks out
of the pupa.

**Baby
ladybirds
have no spots
at first**

Can you remember?

What will climb out
of this chrysalis?

How do male sticklebacks
frighten their enemies?

How big is the Bee
Hummingbird's nest?

Which of these animals will
a tadpole turn into?